THOMAS LUPO

The Six-Part Consort Music

edited by Richard Charteris

CONTENTS

INTRODUCTION iv
LIST OF SOURCES AND THEIR ABBREVIATIONS vi
CRITICAL COMMENTARY viii

SIX-PART CONSORT MUSIC

1	Fantasia	1
2	Fantasia	4
3	Fantasia	8
4	Fantasia	12
5	Fantasia	16
6	Fantasia	20
7	Fantasia	23
8	Fantasia	27
9	Fantasia	30
10	Fantasia	35
11	Fantasia	39
12	Fantasia	42

ISBN-10: 1 898131 05 8; ISBN-13: 9781898131052 © 1993 Fretwork Editions, London
General Editors: Bill Hunt & Julia Hodgson
Reprinted 2020

For Frank A. D'Accone

INTRODUCTION

The details we possess about the life of Thomas Lupo (1571–1627) have been revealed elsewhere,[1] though a few comments here are appropriate. Thomas Lupo was granted a position for life at the English court in 1591 and continued to serve there until his death in 1627. He was acknowledged as 'Composer for the violins' in 1621, though he seems to have occupied the appointment from 1619. As one of the leading instrumental composers of the early seventeenth-century English court, Thomas Lupo — together with John Coprario (d. 1626) and Orlando Gibbons (d. 1625) — was one of the first composers to use violins in serious chamber music and to experiment with new concepts in the design of pieces. All three composers — together with a number of other musicians, including Alfonso Ferrabosco the Younger (d. 1628) — belonged to a group known as 'Coprario's Music'. This group was employed in Prince Charles's household, and later in the main royal household when Charles became king in 1625. From time to time this group of musicians was joined by the royal sovereign on bass viol, and continued to exist well after Coprario's death in 1626. It seems that much of the instrumental music by Lupo and his colleagues was written for performance by 'Coprario's Music'. Indeed, since the earliest source of Lupo's six-part fantasias — London, British Library, Madrigal Society MSS G. 37–42 — almost certainly originated from the English court during Lupo's service there, we have token support for the view that most, possibly all, of the works in the present volume were composed for the royal court.[2]

Although Lupo's six-part fantasias lack instrumental specifications in the original sources, there are good reasons to consider that they were written for viol consort. Apart from the fact that the English consort fantasia was traditionally performed on viols (though certain works require the participation of one or more violins), Lupo's six-part fantasias are preserved in seventeenth-century manuscript sources — none of them autograph — which include viol consort works by other composers. However, the flexible attitude towards instrumentation during Lupo's lifetime must have resulted in these six-part fantasias being performed from time to time on instruments other than viols. Consequently, modern performers should not have any misgivings about using other consort instruments if they wish.

The majority of Lupo's six-part fantasias are written in a conservative style in which imitative ideas, interspersed occasionally with homophonic passages, are given prominence. Notwithstanding this fact, some of Lupo's six-part fantasias are characterized by distinctive features. No. 5 makes more use of homophonic texture than any other piece in the collection, not least in its opening where Lupo avoids the imitative entries that begin his other works in this volume. While imitative entries appear in the opening of Lupo's other six-part fantasias, each piece is distinctive. In the opening of No. 1, for example, it takes ten breve bars before its single, expansive subject achieves an entry in all parts. On the other hand, the opening of No. 6 features two subjects, fast moving ones that engage all parts by the fifth breve bar. The influence of dance music, which is so evident in some of his fantasias and airs for smaller combinations of instruments, is seen in several fantasias in the present volume. Perhaps the most obvious example is No. 4, which is divided into well-defined sections, often contrasted by means of different rhythms and textures, and which uses a double bar line just beyond the halfway point. One could easily imagine the latter piece having been written for the special group of performers that played at the royal court in 'Coprario's Music'. Although Nos. 9 and 10 have no dance-like features, a similar comment could be made about these two pieces. Both works have two bass parts with florid, ornamental writing suitable for the division viol, parts that might well have appealed to some of the expert performers in the royal household. These two fantasias are not as elaborate as the division pieces by later composers, such as William Lawes, John Jenkins and Christopher Simpson, but they represent — together with another two division fantasias by Lupo for five instruments and some similar works by William White — important early examples of the practice in English consort music. Both works feature some fine instrumental writing that will interest more adventurous players.

---

1.   David Lasocki, 'Professional Recorder Playing in England 1500–1700, i: 1500–1640', *Early Music*, 10 (1982), pp. 23–29; Roger Prior, 'Jewish Musicians at the Tudor Court', *The Musical Quarterly*, 69 (1983), pp. 253–265; and Peter Holman, 'The English Royal Violin Consort in the Sixteenth Century', *Proceedings of the Royal Musical Association*, 109 (1982–1983), pp. 39–59. John M. Jennings, 'Lupo, Thomas', *The New Grove Dictionary of Music and Musicians* (London, 1980), xi, pp. 336–337, requires some revision in the light of the findings presented in the previously mentioned articles. The revisions are summarized in Peter Holman's review of *Thomas Lupo: The Two- and Three-Part Consort Music*, ed. Richard Charteris, Boethius Editions 8 (Kilkenny, 1987) in *Chelys*, 17 (1988), pp. 43–47. Additional details about Thomas Lupo are revealed in: Andrew Ashbee, *Records of English Court Music: Volume IV (1603–1625)* (Snodland, Kent, 1991); idem, *Records of English Court Music: Volume V (1625–1714)* (Aldershot, 1991); and Peter Holman, *Four and Twenty Fiddlers: The Violin at the English Court 1540–1690*, Oxford Monographs on Music (Oxford, 1993). Besides the edition of Lupo's two-, and three-part consort music indicated above, the major editions of Thomas Lupo's music include: *Thomas Lupo: The Complete Vocal Music*, ed. Richard Charteris, Boethius Editions 2 (Kilkenny, 1982); and *Thomas Lupo: The Four-Part Consort Music*, ed. Richard Charteris and John M. Jennings, Boethius Editions 4 (Kilkenny, 1983).

2.   For further details about the manuscript source see: Richard Charteris, 'A Rediscovered Source of English Consort Music', *Chelys*, 5 (1973–1974), pp. 3–6.

The order and numbering of the pieces in this volume adhere to the index of these works in Gordon Dodd, *Thematic Index of Music for Viols*, i–ii (London, 1980, 1982). Here numbers 1–10 follow the order of these same pieces in the manuscript score-book, Oxford, Christ Church Library, Music MS 2; the order of the remaining two pieces follows no particular early source. In the absence of autograph sources of Lupo's music, one is obliged to rely on early manuscript copies. In this edition I have used the following sources as the principal ones: for Nos. 1–8 and 12, London, British Library, Madrigal Society MSS G. 37–42; for Nos. 9 and 10, Oxford, Christ Church Library, Music MSS 473–478; and for No. 11, Dublin, Archbishop Marsh's Library, Music MSS Z3. 4. 1–6.

Most performers are familiar with the fact that flexibility in the use of tempo and dynamics are an essential requirement in the performance of this music. Both Thomas Mace and Christopher Simpson remind us that the responsibility lies with the performer to 'humour' the music.[3] It is also useful to remember the guideline of taking each note with a new bow, though some semiquaver passages might benefit from the application of slurs. As in the instrumental music of his English contemporaries, no bowing, dynamic or tempo indications are found in the sources of Lupo's six-part fantasias; similarly, no such indications are supplied in this edition. Nor are there any indications of where performers might employ ornaments, though their use is probably best confined to important cadences.[4]

Like some of Lupo's five-part fantasias, four of his six-part fantasias have reductions of the string parts for organ in the extant manuscript sources. In addition, one of the six-part pieces with a reduction for organ, and four other six-part pieces have a *basso seguente* part in a mid-seventeenth-century keyboard volume. The organ reductions are found in mid-to-late seventeenth-century manuscript sources, like those for some of the fantasias by Alfonso Ferrabosco the Younger and John Coprario. Their absence from early seventeenth-century sources suggests that these were added to suit the taste of performers from the Caroline period onwards, no doubt to act as a '*Holding, Uniting-Constant Friend;* and . . . a *Touch-stone*, to try the certainty of *All Things'*.[5] The mid-seventeenth-century *basso seguente* parts appear in Dublin, Archbishop Marsh's Library, Music MS Z4. 2. 16. This particular manuscript volume also includes a small number of figures that clarify the harmonies of some passages, besides a handful of superscript notes which fill out a chord or elaborate a series of progressions. The organ reductions and *basso seguente* parts are not included in the present edition since they add nothing new to the pieces concerned.

I should like to record my thanks to Bill Hunt and Julia Hodgson of Fretwork Editions for seeing these pieces through the press. In addition, I would like to thank the Australian Research Council for its financial support without which this edition could not have been prepared for publication.

MUSIC DEPARTMENT,   RICHARD CHARTERIS
UNIVERSITY OF SYDNEY,
N.S.W. 2006,
AUSTRALIA.
24 JUNE 1993

---

3. See Thomas Mace, *Musick's Monument* (London, 1676), p. 109; and Christopher Simpson, *The Division Viol* (second edition, London, 1665), p. 10.
4. For details about the ornaments that were used in viol music during this period see: Thurston Dart, 'Ornament Signs in Jacobean Music for Lute and Viol', *The Galpin Society Journal*, 14 (1961), pp. 30–33; Carolyn Coxon, 'Some Notes on English Graces for the Viol', *Chelys*, 2 (1970), pp. 18–22; Mary Cyr, 'A Seventeenth-Century Source of Ornamentation for Voice and Viol: British Museum MS Egerton 2971', *Royal Musical Association Research Chronicle*, 9 (1971), pp. 53–72.
5. Thomas Mace, *ibid.*, p. 242.

LIST OF SOURCES AND THEIR ABBREVIATIONS

Manuscript Sources

Dublin, Archbishop Marsh's Library:

DMa: Z3. 4. 1–6: six part-books which seem to have been one of the copy texts for OBa (dated 1641); compiled in the middle of the seventeenth century and used at Archbishop Narcissus Marsh's music meetings in Oxford before he left for Ireland in 1678.
Relevant works: Nos. 1–5, 8–12.
Literature: Richard Charteris, 'Consort Music Manuscripts in Archbishop Marsh's Library, Dublin', *Royal Musical Association Research Chronicle*, 13 (1976), pp. 27–63; *idem, A Catalogue of the Printed Books on Music, Printed Music and Music Manuscripts in Archbishop Marsh's Library, Dublin*, Boethius Editions 1 (Kilkenny, 1982); John Irving, 'Two Consort Manuscripts from Oxford and Dublin: Their Copying and a Possible Dating', *The Consort*, 42 (1986), pp. 41–49; Richard Charteris, 'New Information about Some of The Consort Music Manuscripts in Archbishop Marsh's Library, Dublin', *The Consort*, 43 (1987), pp. 38–39; *Alfonso Ferrabosco the Younger: Four-Part Fantasias for Viols*, ed. Andrew Ashbee and Bruce Bellingham, Musica Britannica 62 (London, 1992), p. xxv.

DMb: Z4. 2. 16: a keyboard volume with *basso seguente* parts compiled before 1678.
Relevant works: Nos. 1–5.
Literature: See the publications by Charteris and Irving cited above with DMa.

London, The British Library:

LBa: Additional MSS 39550–39554: five part-books which lack a sextus volume; compiled before 1655; one of the hands in these part-books belongs to Sir Nicholas Le Strange (d. 1655).
Relevant works: Nos. 1–11.
Literature: Pamela J. Willetts, 'Sir Nicholas Le Strange and John Jenkins', *Music & Letters*, 42 (1961), pp. 30–43.

LBb: Additional MSS 40657–40661: five part-books which lack a sextus volume; largely copied by William Lawes (d. 1645) with the bookstamp of the Shirley family of Staunton Harrold, Leicestershire, on the covers of each part-book; one of the other hands has contributed to San Marino, Huntington Library, Ellesmere MSS EL 25 A 46–51.
Relevant work: No. 1.
Literature: Richard Charteris, 'The Huntington Library Part Books, Ellesmere MSS EL 25 A 46–51', *The Huntington Library Quarterly*, 50 (1987), pp. 59–84.

LBc: Madrigal Society MSS G. 37–42: six part-books which date from the early seventeenth century; the same hand appears throughout these part-books and is found in Cambridge, Fitzwilliam Museum, Music MU MS 734 (*olim* 24 E 13–17), and in Los Angeles, William Andrews Clark Memorial Library, Music MS fF1995M4.
Relevant works: Nos. 1–8, 12.
Literature: Richard Charteris, 'A Rediscovered Source of English Consort Music', *Chelys*, 5 (1973–1974), pp. 3–6.

Oxford, Bodleian Library:

OBa: MSS Music School C. 64–69: six part-books; each part-book is inscribed 'George Stratford 1641'; largely copied by the main copyist of DMa.
Relevant work: No. 9.
Literature: See the references cited above with DMa.

OBb: MSS Music School E. 437–442: six part-books which date from the mid-seventeenth century; the bulk of the music is copied by an unidentified hand; the other hand belongs to Francis Withey, a later owner, who has signed himself 'F. Withey His Book' on the flyleaf of E. 440.
Relevant work: No. 10.
Literature: Robert Thompson, '"Francis Withie of Oxon" and his Commonplace Book, Christ Church, Oxford, MS 337', *Chelys*, 20 (1991), pp. 3–27.

Oxford, Christ Church Library:

OCa: Music MS 2: a score-book which dates from the mid-seventeenth century; the manuscript was probably copied by Stephen Bing (1610–1681) and once belonged to Christopher, First Baron Hatton (d. 1670).
Relevant works: Nos. 1–10.
Literature: Pamela J. Willetts, 'John Lilly, Musician and Music Copyist', *The Bodleian Library Record*, 7 (1967), pp. 307–311; *idem*, 'Stephen Bing: A Forgotten Violist', *Chelys*, 18 (1989), pp. 3–17; *idem*, 'John Lilly: A Redating', *Chelys*, 21 (1992), pp. 27–38; David Pinto, 'The Music of the Hattons', *Royal Musical Association Research Chronicle*, 23 (1990), pp. 79–108.

OCb: Music MS 44: a score-book which is largely compiled by Thomas Myriell (d. 1625), the rector of St. Stephen's, Walbrook; a few leaves are in the hand of Benjamin Cosyn.
Relevant work: No. 1.
Literature: Pamela J. Willetts, 'Musical Connections of Thomas Myriell', *Music & Letters*, 49 (1968), pp. 36–42; *idem*, 'The Identity of Thomas Myriell', *Music & Letters*, 53, (1972), pp. 431–433; Craig Monson, 'Thomas Myriell's Manuscript Collection: One View of Musical Taste in Jacobean London', *Journal of the American Musicological Society*, 30 (1977), pp. 419–465; and *idem*, *Voices and Viols in England 1600–1650: The Sources and the Music* (Ann Arbor, 1982)

OCc: Music MSS 403–408: six part-books which date from the mid-seventeenth century; this source was copied by John Lilly (d. 1678) and once belonged to Christopher, First Baron Hatton (d. 1670).
Relevant works: Nos. 1–10.
Literature: See the references cited above with OCa.

OCd: Music MSS 423–428: six part-books which date from the first half of the seventeenth century; this source once belonged to John Browne (1608–1691).
Relevant works: Nos. 2–3, 5–8.
Literature: Andrew Ashbee, 'Instrumental Music from the Library of John Browne (1608–1691), Clerk of the Parliaments', *Music & Letters*, 58 (1977), pp. 43–59; Nigel Fortune and Iain Fenlon, 'Music Manuscripts of John Browne (1608–91) and from Stanford Hall, Leicestershire', *Source Materials and the Interpretation of Music: A Memorial Volume to Thurston Dart*, ed. Ian Bent (London, 1981), pp. 155–168.

OCe: Music MS 436: an organ-book which dates from the mid-seventeenth century; the manuscript was probably copied by Stephen Bing (1610–1681) and once belonged to Christopher, First Baron Hatton (d. 1670).
Relevant works: Nos. 6, 8.
Literature: See the references cited above with OCa.

OCf: Music MSS 473–478: six part-books which date from the mid-seventeenth century; this source once belonged to John Browne (1608–1691).
Relevant works: Nos. 1, 4, 9–10.
Literature: See the references cited above with OCd.

OCg: Music MS 1004: an organ-book which dates from the first half of the seventeenth century; this source once belonged to John Browne (1608–1691).
Relevant works: Nos. 2, 7.
Literature: See the references cited above with OCd.

CRITICAL COMMENTARY

Notes on the Critical Commentary

Notational practices of the period have been edited to accord with modern procedures. The editorial method is as follows.

1. Original clefs, key-signatures and time-signatures and the first sounding note of each part are shown on the prefatory staves. No comment is made if the time-signature is omitted or variant. Where the key-signature in the original sources includes the lower and upper octaves of a flat, one of these has been omitted without comment. Each part in the score is preceded by an editorial indication of its tessitura.
2. Original note-values are retained.
3. The final notes of sections and pieces are made to fit the barring, and no comment is made about variants in the sources.
4. Most of the precautionary accidentals in the manuscript sources are retained in this edition; other redundant accidentals have been tacitly omitted. When an accidental appears with the first of a group of repeated notes in the manuscript sources, the accidental is assumed to apply to any consecutive notes which lack an accidental. Obsolete accidentals in the manuscript sources are modernized in the present edition (for example, the use of flats after sharps to denote naturals). Editorial accidentals are placed above the stave. All accidentals follow the modern convention of lasting the whole bar unless cancelled.
5. No expression, phrasing or bowing marks are added in this edition.
6. The sources of each piece are divided into two categories, a principal source (on which the edition here is based) and concordances. All known seventeenth-century sources have been consulted in the preparation of the edition, and the variants are listed in the Commentary.
7. Only contemporary attributions are acknowledged in the list of sources that begins the entry for each piece. Several sources have recent pencilled attributions with Lupo's pieces or in their list of contents, and these are ignored here.
8. Regular barring and bar-numbering are inserted as required. The music is barred according to the breve, even though a number of contemporary copyists prefer semibreve barring. For example, Francis Tregian (d. 1619) uses semibreve barring in his copies of Lupo's five-part fantasias and vocal works found variously in London, Egerton MS 3665 and New York Public Library, Drexel MS 4302. Another contemporary copyist, Thomas Myriell (d. 1625), also uses semibreve barring in his copies of Lupo's five- and six-part fantasias in OCb.
9. The very occasional use of square brackets in the music signifies that the material it encloses is editorial.
10. The critical notes are mostly self-explanatory. Exact pitch is indicated using the Helmholtz system (where middle C is c' and the octaves relevant to the present publication read C–c, c–c', c'–c", c"–c'''). The parts are numbered in Roman numerals, the uppermost part being I. The sources in which a variant occurs are indicated according to the *sigla* in the 'List of Sources and Their Abbreviations'. If a note is tied across the bar then this counts as two notes, so that the tied note in the new bar is designated as note 1.

SIX-PART CONSORT MUSIC

Abbreviations: br = breve; sbr = semibreve; mn = minim; cr = crotchet; qu = quaver; squ = semiquaver; rst = rest

1. Fantasia [VdGS 1]
Principal Source:
LBc (No. 11; 'Tho: Lupo'; untitled)
Concordances:
DMa (No. 37; 'Tho: Lupo'; 'Fantazia')
DMb (No. 22/77; 'Mr Lupo'; 'Fancie'; this *basso seguente* part is ignored here)
LBa (No. 1; 'Tho: Lupo'; 'Fancy'; lacks part VI)
LBb (f. 45r; 'Tho: Lupo'; untitled; lacks part V)
OCa (ff. 214r–215r; unattributed; untitled)
OCb (ff. 113v–116r; unattributed; '180: t[h]e g^t boo[k]^s.' and 'Phantazia'; parts I and II are interchanged)
OCc (ff. 77v–78r; unattributed; untitled)
OCf (No. 3; 'M^r: Lupo'; 'Phantazia')

bar	part	note(s)	comment	bar	part	note(s)	comment
6	II	6	sharp omitted (LBb, OCa, OCb, OCc).	24	IV	2	flat omitted (OCf).
6	VI	4	(to Bar 7, Note 1) tie omitted (OCa, OCb).	24	V	2	(to Bar 26, Note 1) sbr g, br g, sbr g (OCa).
8	V	1	(to Bar 9, Note 1) tie omitted (OCf).	26	I	2	(to Bar 27, Note 1) tie omitted (OCa).
9	V	2	cr f (DMa).	26	III	3	(to Bar 27, Note 1) tie omitted (OCf).
12	VI	1	(to Bar 13, Note 1) tie omitted (OCa, OCb).	26	IV	3	omitted (OCa).
14	VI	6	dotted mn c' (OCb).	26	IV	4	(to Bar 27, Note 1) tie omitted (OCa).
16	V	2–3	dotted qu e, squ d (LBa).	27	III	2–3	sbr f ' (OCf).
18	II	4	flat omitted (OCa).	27	VI	3	(to Bar 28, Note 1) tie omitted (OCa).
19	III	9	flat omitted (OCa).	29	II	1	mn g", cr g" (OCa).
22	IV	8	cr e', cr e' (OCa).	30	IV	1	sharp omitted (OCa).
23	VI	1	sbr d (DMa, OCf).	31	V	1	sbr D (OCa, OCb, OCc).
24	I	3	natural omitted (LBb, LBc, OCa, OCc).	33	IV	2	cr a (LBb, OCa, OCc).

bar	part	note(s)	comment
36	V	1–2	qu a, qu a, qu g, qu f (OCa, CCb, OCc).
38	V	3	(to Bar 39, Note 1) tie omitted (OCa).
40	I	1	sbr e", sbr e" (OCa).
40	IV	1	sbr e', sbr e' (OCa).
40	V	1	sbr c', mn c' (OCa).
45	I	3	sharp omitted (LBb, OCa, OCb, OCc).
47	I	4	(to Bar 48, Note 1) tie omitted (OCa).
47	V	2	sharp omitted (LBa).
50	I	2	sharp omitted (DMa, LBa, LBb, LBc, OCb, OCc).
51	IV	1	sbr d', mn d' (OCa).
57	V	2	sbr a, mn a (OCa).
58	V	2	(to Bar 59, Note 1) tie omitted (OCb).

2. Fantasia [VdGS 2]

Principal Source:
LBc (No. 12; 'Tho: Lupo'; untitled)

Concordances:
DMa (No. 40; 'Tho: Lupo'; 'Fantazia')
DMb (No. 13/78; 'Mr: Lupo'; 'Fancie'; this *basso seguente* part is ignored here)
LBa (No. 4; 'Tho: Lupo'; 'Fancy'; lacks part V)
OCa (ff. 215v–216v; unattributed; untitled)
OCc (ff. 78v–79r; unattributed; untitled)
OCd (No. 35; 'Tho Lupo'; 'Fantazia')
OCg (pp. 140–142 in reverse order; 'Tho: Lupo'; '35 in ye Ruffe bookes' and 'Fantaziae'; this keyboard reduction is ignored here)

bar	part	note(s)	comment
5	VI	cr-rst	mn a is inserted between this and Note 4 (DMa).
6	V	1	(to mn-rest) sbr-rest (DMa, OCd).
8	IV	3	cr d' (DMa).
8	VI	2	cr a (DMa, LBa, OCd).
8	VI	3–4	cr d (DMa, LBa, OCd).
14	IV	1	cr f (DMa, LBa, LBc, OCc).
17	I	3–4	dotted cr a', qu a' (LBa).
17	II	7	(to Bar 18, Note 1) tie omitted (OCa, OCc).
17	IV	2	(plus mn-rest and Note 3) dotted mn a, mn a' (OCa, OCc).
18	VI	1	qu-rest, qu d (OCa, OCc).
19	II	6	mn a', cr-rest (DMa, LBa, OCd).
20	I	3–6	qu f ", qu e", cr d", cr c" sharp (OCd).
20	III	6	sharp omitted (OCa, OCc, OCd).
20	IV	1	(to Bar 22, cr-rest) omitted (OCd).
22	V	5	qu b (OCc).
22	VI	cr-rst	(to Note 7) mn-rest, cr-rest (DMa).
23	III	3	sharp omitted (OCd).
23	III	6	mn d', mn-rest (OCd).
23	VI	9	(to Bar 24, Note 1) mn A, mr-rest (OCa, OCc).
26	IV	2	mn b (DMa).
27	I	4	(to Bar 28, Note 1) tie omitted (DMa).
31	I	1	(to Bar 32, Note 2) erased (DMa).
33	I	2	sharp omitted (OCc).
36	II	5	sharp omitted (DMa, OCa).
39	I	3	(to Bar 40, Note 1) tied (LBa).
45	IV	1	dotted mn g' (OCa, OCc).
48	I	4	cr d" in all sources.
49	I	5	sharp omitted (OCa).
50	I	2	natural omitted (DMa, LBa, OCa, OCc, OCd).
51	II	4	natural omitted (DMa, LBa, OCa, OCd).
53	III	1	mn b' (DMa).
57	V	7	flat omitted (DMa, LBc, OCd).
59	VI	1	mn c (OCa, OCc).
62	V	2–4	flat omitted (OCd).
65	III	4–6	cr f ', qu d', qu d" (OCa, OCc).
65	III	7–8	cr c", cr a' (LBc).
65	III	8	qu b' (DMa).
66	V	1	mn a, mn a (DMa).

3. Fantasia [VdGS 3]

Principal Source:
LBc (No. 18; 'Tho: Lupo'; untitled)

Concordances:
DMa (No. 44; 'Tho: Lupo'; 'Fantazia')
DMb (No. 15; 'Mr: Lupo'; 'Fancie'; this *basso seguente* part is ignored here)
LBa (No. 6; 'Tho: Lupo'; 'Fancy'; lacks part V)
OCa (ff. 217r–217v; unattributed; untitled)
OCc (ff. 79v–80r; unattributed; untitled)
OCd (No. 37; 'Tho. Lupo'; 'Fantazia')

As the information below reveals, the music from the second half of bar 4 to the end of bar 17 in OCd is substantially different from that in the other sources.

bar	part	note(s)	comment
2	V	4	sharp omitted (OCc).
2	V	6	sharp omitted (OCa, OCc).
3	IV	cr-rst	cr a (DMa).
3	IV	cr-rst	(to Note 4) qu-rest, qu g', qu f ', qu e' (OCd).
3	V	8	sharp omitted (OCd).
4	I	4	(to Bar 7, sbr-rest) dotted sbr e", dotted mn e", qu d" sharp, qu e", mn f " sharp, mn g", mn e", mn d", dotted cr c", qu b', qu a', qu b , qu c", qu d", sbr e", mn-rest (OCd).
4	IV	4	(to Bar 6, br-rest) mn e', dotted cr e', qu d', cu c', qu b, cr a, dotted cr a', qu g', mn f ' sharp, cr-rest, qu d', qu c', mn b, sbr g, mn a (OCd).
4	V	4	(to Bar 6, Note 1) br e, sbr-rest, sor-rest (OCd).
5	V	2	cr f sharp (OCa).
6	III	2	(to Bar 8, Note 2) cr c", cr c', dotted cr d', qu e', qu f ', qu e', cr a', mn c", mn-rest, sbr-rest, sbr-rest (OCd).

bar	part	note(s)	comment	bar	part	note(s)	comment
7	II	4–6	dotted cr c", qu e", qu d" sharp, qu e", cr f" sharp (OCd).	16	V	1	(to mn-rest) br-rest (OCd).
7	IV	4–6	qu g' sharp, qu f' sharp, qu g' sharp (OCd).	19	IV	cr-rst	(to Note 1) mn g (DMa, LBa, OCa, OCc).
7	IV	5	sharp omitted (OCc).	20	II	mn-rst	cr-rest, cr e' (OCd).
7	IV	9	(to Bar 12, Note 1) qu f ' sharp, qu e', cr d' sharp, mn e', cr c' sharp, mn e', cr d', mn c' sharp, mn b, dotted mn g, cr d', cr c', cr b, dotted mn c', cr d', cr e', cr d', mn e', cr-rest, cr d', mn d', sbr d', sbr-rest (OCd).	23	II	2	(to Bar 24, Note 3) cr d", dotted cr c", qu d", cr e", qu f ", qu d", dotted cr g", qu f ", qu e", qu e", cr d", mn c" (DMa, LBa, OCa, OCc).
8	II	3–4	cr b', mn a' sharp (OCd).	23	III	1	(to Bar 24, Note 2) qu e', qu c', cr d', cr e', cr f ', qu g', qu g, qu a, qu b, mn c', mn e' (DMa; with the exception of cr e' and cr f ' which read as dotted cr e' and qu f ', also in LBa, OCa, OCc; though the final note — mn e' — is mn g' in OCa, OCc).
8	II	4	sharp omitted (OCa, OCc).				
9	II	3	(to Bar 13, Note 1) cr d", cr g", dotted cr g", qu f ", dotted mn e", cr d", cr c" sharp, mn d", cr c" sharp, dotted sbr d", sbr e", mn d", cr c", dotted cr c", qu a' (OCd).				
				23	IV	1	(to Bar 24, Note 2) cr g' natural, cr g', mn a', cr g', cr f ', qu e', qu c', qu e', qu d', cr c', cr b (DMa, LBb, OCa, OCc).
9	VI	2	(to sbr-rest) cr c, qu B, qu A, mn G, mn-rest (OCd).	23	V	8–9	mn c, cr d (OCd).
10	I	5	(to Bar 11, Note 2) dotted cr e', qu d' (OCd).	24	III	3	mn e' (OCa, OCc).
10	IV	3–5	mn d', cr c' sharp, mn d' (DMa).	24	IV	1–2	cr c', cr b (OCd).
11	III	4	(to Bar 13, Note 1) mn b' natural, mn g', dotted mn e' natural, cr c', cr d', cr g', cr e', dotted cr f ', qu e' (OCd).	24	V	1–4	cr c, cr G (OCd).
				26	VI	br-rst	sbr-rest (LBc).
13	I	6	sharp omitted (OCd).	27	I	6	flat omitted (OCd).
14	III	cr-rst	cr d' (OCd).	27	VI	4	sharp omitted (DMa, LBa, LBc, OCd).
15	I	6	(to Bar 17, Note 3) sbr b', dotted mn b', cr d", sbr c" [without sharp], cr b', cr g', mn c" (OCd).	29	II	2	flat omitted (DMa).
				30	IV	2	cr c' (OCd).
15	III	1	(to Bar 17, Note 5) br-rest, mn-rest, cr b, qu b, qu c', qu d', qu c', qu d', qu b, dotted cr c', qu d', qu e', qu f ', dotted cr g', qu a', qu b', qu c", sbr a' (OCd).	31	VI	4	(to Bar 32, Note 2) dotted sbr d (OCd).
				31	VI	5	cr A (DMa).
				32	VI	1–2	sbr d (OCa, OCc).
15	III	2	dotted mn b (OCa, OCc).	35	V	6	natural omitted (DMa, LBc).
15	IV	4	(to Bar 17, Note 1) dotted sbr e', dotted cr d' sharp, qu e', cr f ' sharp, cr b', cr a', cr a, qu c', qu d', cr e', cr b, cr e' (OCd).	37	III	2	sharp omitted (OCa).
				38	I	2	sharp omitted (OCa, OCc).
				39	I	5	cr b' (OCa, OCc).
				40	III	3	sharp omitted (OCa, OCc).
15	VI	1	(to Bar 17, Note 1) mn a, dotted mn a, cr A, mn e, sbr B, cr B, cr G, dotted mn A (OCd).	41	I	6–8	dotted cr c" [without sharp], qu d" (OCa, OCc).
				42	I	2	sharp omitted (OCa, OCc).
16	I	5	(to Bar 18, Note 1) natural omitted (DMa).	42	VI	2	sharp omitted (OCd).
16	V	1–2	dotted mn b, cr a (OCa, OCc).	47	V	3	(to Bar 48, Note 1) tie omitted (OCa).

4. Fantasia [VdGS 4]

Principal Source:
LBc (No. 16; 'Tho: Lupo'; untitled)
Concordances:
DMa (No. 38; 'Tho: Lupo'; 'Fantazia')
DMb (No. [16]; 'M^r: Lupo'; 'Fancie'; lacks bars 32–62; this *basso seguente* part is ignored here)
LBa (No. 3; 'Tho: Lupo', 'Fancy'; lacks part V)
OCa (ff. 218r–219r; unattributed; untitled)
OCc (ff. 80v–81r; unattributed, untitled)
OCf (No. 4; 'M^r: Lupo'; 'Phantazia')

bar	part	note(s)	comment	bar	part	note(s)	comment
5	III	1	sharp omitted (LBa).				sources, LBa, also has a fermata sign with each of the notes — except in part V which is missing from this source.
6	I	3	cr d" sharp (LBa, OCa, OCc).				
13	III	1	sharp omitted (LBa).				
14	II	1	sbr g" sharp (LBa, OCa).	34	VI	1	br E (OCa).
15	VI	2	natural omitted (LBa, OCa, OCc).	40	III	3	cr g' sharp (LBa, OCa).
17	II	10	(to Bar 18, Note 1) dotted cr d" (OCa, OCc).	41	VI	3	(to Bar 42, Note 1) sharp omitted (LBa).
17	V	8	cr c (OCc).	47	I	5	mn f ' sharp (LBa, OCa).
17	VI	2	cr B (OCf).	47	II	2	natural omitted (LBa).
21	I	2–3	dotted sbr e" (DMa, LBa, OCc, OCf).	47	III	2	natural omitted (DMa).
23	I	2	sharp omitted (OCa, OCc).	47	IV	3	mn f sharp (OCa).
25	I	7	sharp omitted (OCa, OCc).	53	VI	6	natural omitted (DMa).
28	V	6	sharp omitted (OCa, OCc).	54	III	1	flat omitted (OCa).
28	VI	7	qu g sharp (OCf).	54	III	1	(to Bar 55, Note 3) cr c", cr b' flat, cr g', sbr a', mn a', mn-rest (DMa).
31	V	4	sharp omitted (DMa, OCa, OCc)/				
31	VI	8	sharp omitted (OCa, OCc).	54	III	3	cr g' (DMa, LBa).
32	II	5	mn c" (OCf).	55	I	2–3	mn d", cr c" sharp (DMa, LBa, OCf).
33	I	4	cr c" (OCa, OCc).	58	V	1	natural omitted (DMa, OCa, OCc).
34	I–VI	dbl bar	double barline appears in all sources; one of the	59	IV	6	cr g' sharp (OCf).

5. Fantasia [VdGS 5]

Principal Source:
LBc (No. 15; 'Tho: Lupo'; untitled)
Concordances:
DMa (No. 42; 'Tho: Lupo'; 'Fantazia')
DMb (No. [14]/79; 'Mr: Lupo'; 'Fancie'; this *basso seguente* is ignored here)
LBa (No. 2; 'Tho: Lupo'; 'Fancy'; lacks part VI)
OCa (ff. 219v–220v; unattributed; untitled)
OCc (ff. 81v–82r; unattributed; untitled)
OCd (No. 36; 'Tho. Lupo'; 'Fantazia')

bar	part	note(s)	comment
3	I	3	(to Bar 4, Note 2) sbr e", br e' (OCa).
3	IV	1	(to Bar 4, Note 1) tie omitted (OCa).
5	V	1	mn b, mn b (OCa).
5	V	2	(to Bar 6, Note 1) mn e, mn a, mn d, sbr g (OCa, OCc, OCd).
9	V	1	mn f (DMa).
10	V	4	natural omitted (LBa, LBc, OCc, OCd).
13	I	2	mn e" (DMa).
17	I	4	(to Bar 15, Note 1) tied (OCa, OCc, OCd).
20	III	2	cr g' sharp (OCd).
25	II	3	cr e" (LBa); cr g" (OCa, OCc).
33	VI	1	cr f (LBc).
45	VI	6–11	qu g, qu G, dotted cr g, qu e, dotted cr g sharp, qu g (OCa); qu g, qu G, dotted cr g, qu e, qu g sharp, qu g, qu g, qu g (OCc).
45	VI	8	dotted cr f sharp (DMa).
51	III	2–3	omitted (LBc, OCd).
54	VI	3	sharp omitted (OCa, OCc).
55	I	5	natural omitted (DMa, OCa, OCc).
60	II	3–6	qu f ", qu e", dotted mn e" (OCd).
61	I	9	sharp omitted (OCa).
61	III	4–6	dotted cr e' (DMa, LBa); dotted cr f ' [without sharp] (OCa, OCc).
61	III	7	sharp omitted (OCa, OCc).

6. Fantasia [VdGS 6]

Principal Source:
LBc (No. 9; 'Tho: Lupo'; untitled)
Concordances:
LBa (No. 7; 'Tho: Lupo'; 'Fancy'; lacks part V)
OCa (ff. 221r–222r; unattributed; untitled)
OCc (ff. 82v–83r; unattributed; untitled)
OCd (No. 38; 'Tho: Lupo'; 'Fantazia')
OCe (ff. 147v–148r; unattributed; untitled; this keyboard reduction is ignored here)

bar	part	note(s)	comment
1–2	II		omitted (OCd).
6	VI	4	omitted (OCd).
8	I	3	natural omitted (LBc).
8	I	7	flat omitted (LBa, LBc, OCc, OCd).
9	III	3	sharp omitted (LBa).
10	IV	4	natural omitted (OCd).
11	I	1	(to Bar 12, Note 1) mn-rest, cr a", cr g", mn f " (LBa).
11	V	9	sharp omitted (OCa, OCc, OCd).
12	VI	9	sharp omitted (OCa, OCc).
14	I	3	qu g" (OCd).
14	III	4	flat omitted (LBa, LBc).
15	I	4	sbr c" (LBc).
15	II	mn-rst	(to sbr-rest) mn g", mn f ", mn-rest (OCa, OCc, OCd).
15	III	2	dotted cr g', qu e' (OCd).
15	IV	4–5	dotted cr e', qu d', qu e', qu g' (OCd).
15	VI	3	qu b (OCa, OCc).
17	II	6	(to Bar 18, Note 2) mn e", mn d", sbr c" (OCd).
17	IV	7	flat omitted (OCd).
18	I	6	(to Bar 19, Note 2) mn e" (OCa, OCc, OCd).
18	II	3	(to Bar 20, br-rest) mn c", dotted mn c", cr d", qu e", qu f ", mn g", cr a", mn g", cr f ", cr c", sbr d", mn-rest (OCd).
18	III	3	(to Bar 20, Note 6) cr e', mn c', mn c", mn a', cr b' natural, mn c", dotted mn c", mn a', cr b', mn a', mn d' (OCd).
19	I	4	sharp omitted (OCa, OCc).
19	IV	3	qu f ', qu e' (LBa, OCd).
20	I	1	mn c" (OCd).
20	IV	6	(to Bar 21, Note 1) dotted cr b natural, qu b natural (LBa, OCa, OCc).
21	V	1–3	cr E, mn e, cr f sharp (OCd).
21	I	6–7	mn c" (OCd).
21	I	7	natural omitted (LBa, OCa, OCc).
21	I	8	natural omitted (LBa, OCa, OCc, OCd).
23	I	1	sharp omitted (LBa, OCa, OCc, OCd).
23	VI	2	(to Bar 24 Note 1) qu d, qu e, qu f, qu g, mn a, cr-rest (LBc).
24	V	2	cr e (OCa, OCc, OCd).
25	IV	1	sharp omitted (OCa, OCc, OCd).
25	IV	9	sharp omitted (OCc).
36	V	3	sharp omitted (OCd).
38	VI	3	sharp omitted (OCa, OCc).
39	II	cr-rst	(to Note 5) mn c" (OCd).
42	III	2	cr f ' (LBa).
42	IV	4	qu a, qu a' (LBa, OCd).
43	I	5–6	mn d" (OCa, OCc, OCd).
43	V	2	sharp omitted (OCd).
48	I	4	natural omitted (OCa).
48	VI	1	sharp omitted (OCd).
48	VI	3	natural omitted (OCd).
49	I	5–6	qu a", qu a' (LBc).
51	IV	7	sharp omitted (OCc).
51	V	3–4	dotted mn d (OCa).

7. Fantasia [VdGS 7]

Principal Source:
LBc (No. 10; 'Tho: Lupo'; untitled)
Concordances:
LBa (No. 8; 'Tho: Lupo'; 'Fancy'; lacks part V)
OCa (ff. 222v–223r; unattributed; untitled)
OCc (ff. 83v–84r; unattributed; untitled)
OCd (No. 33; 'Tho: Lupo'; 'Fantazia')
OCg (pp. 143–145 in reverse order; 'Thomas Lupo'; '33 in the Ruff bookes' and 'Fantaziae'; this keyboard reduction is ignored here)

bar	part	note(s)	comment
6	I	4	sharp omitted (OCa, OCc).
9	VI	4	natural omitted (OCa, OCc).
19	IV	1	(to Bar 20, Note 1) tie omitted (OCa, OCc).
26	VI	6	cr F sharp (OCa, OCc).
31	I&II		(to bar 50) these parts are interchanged (OCa, OCc).
31	III	4	cr d' (LBa, OCc); omitted (OCa).
34	IV	4	natural omitted (OCa).
41	II	5	qu d" (OCa, OCc).
43	V	2	mn g sharp (OCa, OCc).
44	IV	9	qu b natural (OCd).
46	VI	1	(to mn-rest) sbr d (LBa, LBc, OCa, OCc).

8. Fantasia [VdGS 8]

Principal Source:
LBc (No. 4; 'Tho: Lupo'; untitled)
Concordances:
DMa (No. 39; 'Tho: Lupo'; 'Fantazia')
LBa (No. 5; 'Tho: Lupo'; 'Fancy'; lacks part V)
OCa (ff. 223v–224v; unattributed; untitled)
OCc (ff. 84v–85r; unattributed; untitled)
OCd (No. 30; 'Tho: Lupo'; 'Fantazia')
OCe (ff. 149v–150r; unattributed; untitled; this keyboard reduction is ignored here)

bar	part	note(s)	comment
8	II	1–2	cr d', mn e' (DMa).
8	III	1–3	sbr-rest, mn-rest (OCa, OCc).
8	V	1–2	sbr G (DMa).
10	II	2	sbr-rest (OCa, OCc).
10	VI	5	qu A flat (LBa).
15	III	4	(to Bar 16, Note 1) cr a' flat, mn g' (LBa).
16	I	sbr-rst	mn d", mn-rest (LBa).
19	III	1–2	dotted sbr g' (DMa, LBa).
19	IV	4	natural omitted (LBa, OCa, OCc).
20	II	2–3	dotted cr f ", qu e" flat (LBa).
20	II	3	flat omitted (OCa, OCc).
20	III	2–3	cr f ', cr e' flat (OCa, OCc).
21	I	4	(to Bar 22, Note 2) dotted mn f " (OCa).
22	III	4	natural omitted (OCa).
22	V	5	flat omitted (OCa).
23	III	1	natural omitted (OCa, OCc, OCd).
23	VI	1–2	br c (LBa).
25	III	2	flat omitted (LBa).
29	IV	5	sharp omitted (OCc).
30	III	3	(to mn-rest) sbr d' (LBa).
32	IV	3	(to Bar 33, first mn-rest) mn-rest, dotted mn g', qu f ', qu e', mn d' (LBa).
35	II	2	(to Bar 36, Note 1) dotted cr g", qu f " (LBa).
35	III	1–2	dotted mn e', mn d' (OCa).
37	IV	br-rst	sbr-rest, cr-rest, cr d', cr c', cr a (OCa, OCc).
37	VI	mn-rst	omitted (OCd).
37	VI	2	cr-rest, cr b flat (OCa, OCc).
38	II	1–2	mn d', mn e' (LBa).
43	III	6	flat omitted (OCa, OCc).
48	I	5	(to Bar 49, Note 2) br b' flat (OCa, OCc).
55	V	1	sbr f (OCd).
59	IV	1	mn-rest, mn g' (OCa, OCc).
60	III	3	natural omitted (DMa, LBa, LBc, OCc, OCd).
60	IV	2	cr g (OCa, OCc).
60	V	1–2	sbr c, cr c (OCa, OCc).

9. Fantasia [VdGS 9]

Principal Source:
OCf (No. 5; 'M^r: Lupo'; untitled except for 'Division Basses')
Concordances:
DMa (No. 22; 'Tho: Lupo'; 'Fantazia')
LBa (No. 9; 'Tho: Lupo'; 'Fancy'; lacks part VI)
OBa (No. 33; 'M^r: Lupo'; untitled)
OCa (ff. 225r–227r; unattributed; untitled)
OCc (ff. 85v–86r; unattributed; untitled)

bar	part	note(s)	comment
5	V	2	sharp omitted (OBa).
7	V	5	(to Bar 8, Note 1) dotted mn a, mn A (DMa, LBa).
7	VI	8	sharp omitted (OBa).
9	III	3	sharp omitted (OBa).

bar	part	note(s)	comment
13	VI	9	sharp omitted (DMa, OBa, OCa, OCc).
14	VI	6	sharp omitted (DMa, OBa, OCa, OCc).
15	II	2	sharp omitted (OBa).
15	II	4	sharp omitted (DMa, OBa).
16	II	4	sharp omitted (DMa, OBa).
16	V	4	preceded by an extra qu d' (LBa).
17	I	3	(to Bar 18, Note 1) tie omitted (OCa).
17	II	1	(to Bar 18, Note 1) mn e'', cr g'', cr a'', mn g'', sbr a'' (OCa).
17	II	1–2	mn e'', dotted mn g'' (LBa).
17	VI	5	squ f sharp (OCa).
17	VI	7	qu f sharp (OCa).
17	VI	9–10	qu e, qu f sharp, qu d, qu c (OBa).
18	IV	3	(to Bar 20, Note 1) sbr g', mn f ' sharp, dotted mn e, cr d', mn c', mn c' (OCa).
18	VI	8–15	these notes are given as demisqus (OBa); another beam has been added by a later hand to make these notes demisqus in (DMa).
21	II	2	mn e'' (LBa).
22	VI	6	sharp omitted (OBa).
23	V	11	sharp omitted (OBa, OCa, OCc); squ f natural (DMa, LBa); squ f (OCf).
23	VI	8	sharp omitted (OCa).
23	VI	10	sharp omitted (OCc).
27	VI	5	sharp omitted (OBa).
27	VI	9	sharp omitted from all sources.
28	V	3	sharp omitted (OBa).
28	VI	12	sharp omitted (DMa, OBa).
28	VI	14	sharp omitted (OCf).
29	II	3	qu c'', qu d'' (DMa, OBa).
29	III	2	qu b (DMa, OCf).
29	V	1–12	qu c', qu a, qu b, qu a, qu g sharp, qu a, qu b, qu g sharp, qu a, qu b, qu g, qu a, cr b, cr a (OBa).
29	V	9	natural omitted (DMa, LBa, OBa).
31	II	3	sharp omitted (DMa, OBa).
32	III	1–3	qu a', qu a', cr a' (LBa).
36	III	1	sharp omitted (DMa, OBa, OCc, OCf).
36	VI	3	mn d (OBa).
37	V	11–18	these notes are given as squs in (OCc).
38	III	5	cr d' (OBa, OCc).
40	VI	17	sharp omitted (OBa, OCa, OCc).
41	III	3	dotted cr c' sharp (DMa, OBa).
42	VI	8	qu G (OBa).
43	I	3	cr a', cr a' (DMa, OBa).
45	II	3	sharp omitted (DMa); mn g'' sharp (OBa).
45	III	3	cr g' (OCf).
47	II	2	(to Bar 48, Note 2) sbr c'', br c'' (OCa).
49	IV	2	cr c' (OBa).
54	VI	1	natural omitted (DMa, OBa, OCc, OCf).
55	III	3	sharp misplaced on previous note (OBa).
55	IV	1	sharp omitted (LBa).
56	II	2	sharp omitted (DMa, OBa); sharp supplied with note 3.
57	IV	1	mn g (LBa).
61	I	7	sharp omitted (DMa, OBa).

10. Fantasia [VdGS 10]

Principal Source:
OCf (No. 6; 'Mr: Lupo'; untitled except for 'Devision Basses')
Concordances:
DMa (No. 23; 'Tho: Lupo'; 'Fantazia')
LBa (No. 10; 'Tho: Lupo'; 'Fancy'; lacks part VI)
OBb (No. 4; 'Mr Lupo'; 'Fantazia')
OCa (ff. 227v–228v; unattributed; untitled)
OCc (ff. 86v–87r; unattributed; untitled)

bar	part	note(s)	comment
3	IV	5	sharp omitted (OBb).
6	VI	2	(to Bar 7, Note 1) tie omitted (OCa, OCc, OCf).
8	II	6	note lacks ledger line (OCf).
8	III	1	sharp omitted (OCf).
8	III	3	sharp omitted (OCa, OCb).
10	IV	2	dotted cr c' sharp (OBb).
10	V	1	changed to sbr c (OBb).
11	I	3	sharp omitted (OBb).
11	V	3rd cr-rst	omitted (OBb).
12	V	9	omitted (OBb).
12	V	12–13	squ f [without sharp], squ e (OBb).
13	VI	6	omitted (OBb).
13	VI	7–8	squ f [without sharp], squ g (OBb).
16	I	2	sharp omitted (OBb).
16	I	6	qu b' (DMa, LBa).
16	IV	5	qu f ' sharp (OCa); qu f [without sharp] (OCc).
19	IV	3	note repeated (OBb).
20	V	10	cr c' (OBb).
20	VI	5–6	squ e, squ d, squ c (OBb).
21	V	15	sharp omitted (OCa, OCc).
22	I	4	(to Bar 23, Note 2) qu b', qu a', cr e'' (LBa, OCa, OCc, OCf).
23	III	3	qu f ' (DMa, OCf).
24	V	13	sharp omitted (OBb, OCa).
24	VI	3	sharp omitted (OCa, OCc).
24	VI	16	sharp misplaced on previous note (OBb).
25	III	2nd cr-rst	(to Note 5) cr-rest, mn f ', mn g' (OBb).
25	IV	4	qu c' (LBa).
25	IV	5	qu d' (LBa, OBb, OCa, OCc).
25	V	19	squ A (OBb).
25	VI	3	qu A (OCf).
25	VI	11	sharp omitted (DMa, OCa).
26	I	cr-rst	(to Bar 38, Note 5) omitted (OBb).
26	II	6	(to Bar 38, Note 4) omitted (OBb).
26	III	4	(to Bar 38, Note 3) omitted (OBb).
26	IV	3	2nd half of Note 3 to Bar 38, Note 4: omitted (OBb).
26	V	2nd cr-rst	(to Bar 38, Note 7) omitted (OBb).
26	VI	5	(to Bar 38, Note 13) omitted (OBb).
26	VI	9	sharp omitted (DMa, OCf).
27	IV	2–3	sbr d (LBa).
27	V	5	sharp omitted (OCa, OCc, OCf).
27	VI	13	sharp omitted (OCa).
27	VI	17–18	omitted (DMa).
27	VI	19	sharp omitted (OCa, OCc).
27	VI	21	sharp omitted (DMa).
27	VI	23	sharp omitted (OCa, OCc, OCf).
28	III	4	qu f ' (DMa, OCa, OCc, OCf).
28	VI	7	sharp omitted (OCa, OCc).
28	VI	19	sharp omitted (DMa).
29	I	5	(to Bar 30, Note 2) dotted mn d'', cr d'', sbr d'' (LBa).

bar	part	note(s)	comment
30	V	1	sharp omitted (DMa).
30	VI	11	sharp omitted (OCa).
31	VI	6	sharp omitted (DMa, OCa, OCc).
33	IV	1	sharp omitted (LBa).
33	IV	2	sharp omitted (LBa).
33	VI	2–3	squ f sharp, squ e (DMa).
33	VI	15	sharp omitted (OCa, OCf).
33	VI	20	sharp omitted (OCc).
34	II	2	cr a' sharp (LBa).
34	III	2	sharp omitted (OCc).
34	IV	2	sharp omitted (DMa).
34	V	15	sharp omitted (OCa).
34	V	17 & 19	sharp omitted (OCc).
35	III	1	cr g (DMa).
35	III	3	sharp omitted (DMa, OCa, OCc, OCf).
35	V	1	sharp omitted (OCc).
35	VI	qu-rst	omitted (DMa).
35	VI	9	qu g sharp (OCa, OCc).
36	I	3	sharp omitted (OCf).
36	V	10	sharp omitted (OCc).
36	VI	8	sharp omitted (OCf).
36	VI	14	sharp omitted (DMa, OCc).
36	VI	17	sharp omitted (DMa, OCf).
37	III	2	cr a (OCf).
37	V	5	sharp omitted (OCa, OCc).
37	V	7	sharp omitted (OCa, OCc, OCf).
37	V	15	sharp omitted (DMa, OCa, OCc).
37	VI	7	sharp omitted (OCc, OCf).
37	VI	9	sharp omitted (OCf).
37	VI	14	sharp omitted (DMa).
38	III	4	dotted mn a' (OBb).
38	V	13 & 17	sharp omitted (OBb).
38	VI	13	cr A sharp (DMa).
40	II	3	natural omitted (OBb).
40	III	7	sharp omitted (OCa).
41	III	2	sharp omitted (OCa).

42 - 46   OBb has the following variant reading for all parts:

47	III	1	sharp omitted (OBb).

11. Fantasia [VdGS 11]

Principal Source:
DMa (No. 43; 'Tho: Lupo'; 'Fantazia')
Concordance:
LBa (No. 11; 'Tho: Lupo'; 'Fancy'; lacks part V)

18	I	7	natural supplied (DMa, LBa).
42	II	4	sharp omitted (DMa).

12. Fantasia [VdGS 12]

Principal Source:
LBc (No. 19; 'Tho: Lupo'; untitled)
Concordance:
DMa (No. 41; 'Tho: Lupo'; 'Fantazia')

6	III	3	cr g (LBc).
39	III	2	flat omitted (DMa).

1. Fantasia

© 1993 Fretwork Editions FE9 Thomas Lupo, The Six-Part Consort Music edited by Richard Charteris

2. Fantasia

© 1993 Fretwork Editions FE9   Thomas Lupo, The Six-Part Consort Music edited by Richard Charteris

8

3. Fantasia

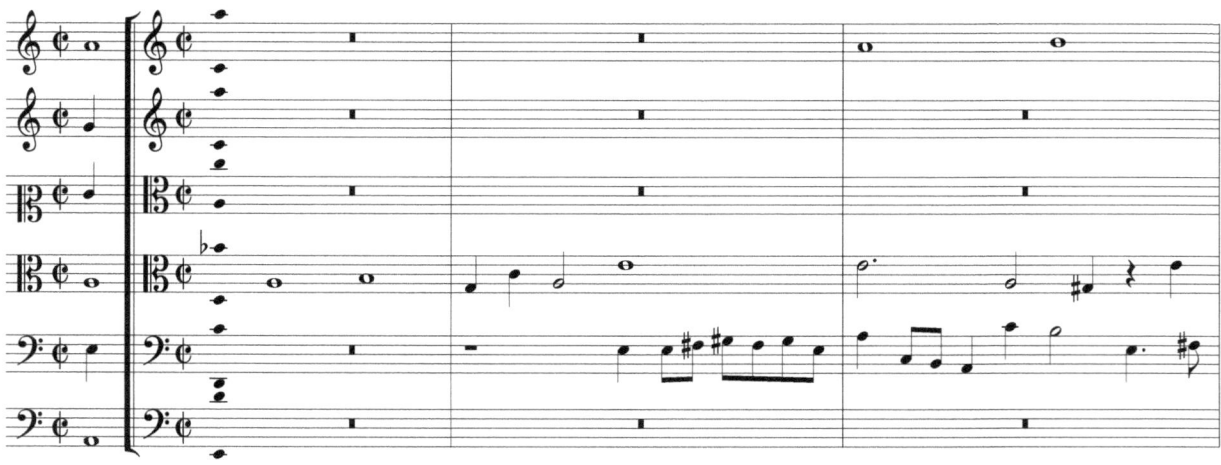

© 1993 Fretwork Editions FE9   Thomas Lupo, The Six-Part Consort Music edited by Richard Charteris

© 1993 Fretwork Editions FE9   Thomas Lupo, The Six-Part Consort Music edited by Richard Charteris

4. Fantasia

© 1993 Fretwork Editions FE9   Thomas Lupo, The Six-Part Consort Music edited by Richard Charteris

5. Fantasia

© 1993 Fretwork Editions FE9   Thomas Lupo, The Six-Part Consort Music edited by Richard Charteris

© 1993 Fretwork Editions FE9   Thomas Lupo, The Six-Part Consort Music edited by Richard Charteris

6. Fantasia

© 1993 Fretwork Editions FE9   Thomas Lupo, The Six-Part Consort Music edited by Richard Charteris

23

7. Fantasia

© 1993 Fretwork Editions FE9   Thomas Lupo, The Six-Part Consort Music edited by Richard Charteris

24

8. Fantasia

© 1993 Fretwork Editions FE9   Thomas Lupo, The Six-Part Consort Music edited by Richard Charteris

© 1993 Fretwork Editions FE9   Thomas Lupo, The Six-Part Consort Music edited by Richard Charteris

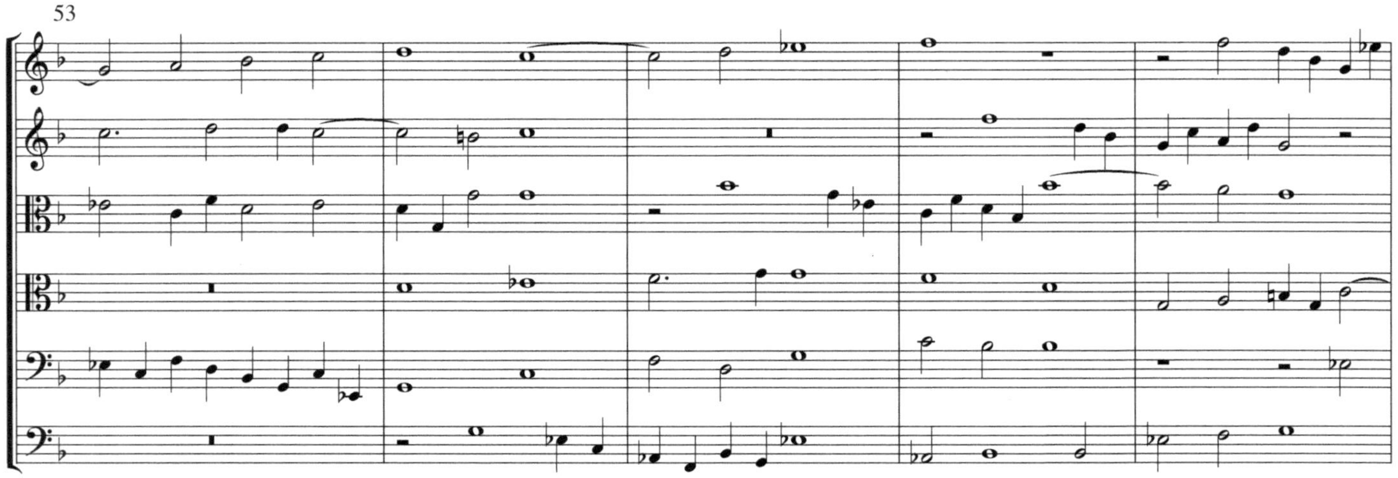

9. Fantasia

10. Fantasia

11. Fantasia

© 1993 Fretwork Editions FE9   Thomas Lupo, The Six-Part Consort Music edited by Richard Charteris

12. Fantasia

www.ingramcontent.com/pod-product-compliance
Lightning Source LLC
Chambersburg PA
CBHW042017090526
44588CB00024B/2891